gathered into one

DEVOTIONS FOR LENT
2024

AUGSBURG FORTRESS

Minneapolis

GATHERED INTO ONE

Devotions for Lent 2024

Scripture quotations are from the New Revised Standard Version Bible, copyright © 1989 by the Division of Christian Education of the National Council of the Churches of Christ in the USA. Used by permission. All rights reserved.

References to ELW are from *Evangelical Lutheran Worship*, copyright © 2006 Evangelical Lutheran Church in America. References to ACS are from *All Creation Sings*, copyright © 2020 Augsburg Fortress, an imprint of 1517 Media.

pISBN 978-1-5064-9659-7
eISBN 978-1-5064-9661-0

Writers: Yolanda Denson-Byers (February 14–18), Phil Ruge-Jones (February 19–27), Jessica Davis (February 28–March 4), Michael Rinehart (March 5–12), Lydia Posselt (March 13–21), Troy M. Troftgruben (March 22–30)

Editor: Laurie J. Hanson

Cover design: Alisha Lofgren

Cover and interior images: All images © Getty Images. Used by permission.

Interior design and typesetting: Eileen Engebretson

The paper used in this publication meets the minimum requirements of American National Standard for Information Sciences—Permanence of Paper for Printed Library Materials, ANSI Z329.48-1984.

Printed in China.

24   23   1   2   3   4   5

Welcome

Gathered into One provides daily devotions for each day from Ash Wednesday to the Resurrection of Our Lord/Vigil of Easter (traditionally known as Holy Saturday). Devotions begin with an evocative image and a brief passage from 1 Corinthians. The writers then bring their diverse voices and pastoral wisdom to the texts with quotations to ponder, reflections, and prayers.

Portions of 1 Corinthians appear in the Revised Common Lectionary during each lectionary year. The apostle Paul writes this letter to the church in Corinth after hearing of quarreling and divisions among the people. He teaches the Corinthians that each person has a unique set of gifts from the Holy Spirit, given for the common good, and reminds them that the church is the body of Christ, joined together with one bread, one cup, one baptism, one God, and one Spirit. This theme of unity amid diversity is as timely now as it was when Paul wrote to the Corinthians.

During this journey through Lent to the Easter feast, may we celebrate the diversity among us as well our unity in Christ.

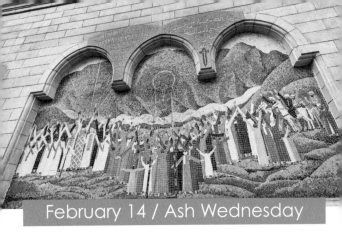

February 14 / Ash Wednesday

1 Corinthians 1:1-3

Paul, called to be an apostle of Christ Jesus by the will of God, and our brother Sosthenes,

To the church of God that is in Corinth, to those who are sanctified in Christ Jesus, called to be saints, together with all those who in every place call on the name of our Lord Jesus Christ, both their Lord and ours:

Grace to you and peace from God our Father and the Lord Jesus Christ.

To ponder

Life is full of awe and grace and truth, mystery and wonder. I live in that atmosphere.—Dion DiMucci, in "Dion Is Still a New York Guy at Heart"

Common ground

Today is Ash Wednesday, when we remember our Savior and our common humanity as we confess our sin and receive the forgiveness of Almighty God. Christians around the world will hear the words, "Remember that you are dust, and to dust you shall return." We will encounter siblings in Christ with dust upon their brows and greet one another, in love and humility, recognizing that our human bodies are frail and we are all destined to become dust once again.

When Paul wrote to the church at Corinth, he first reminded the people of their unity with all Christians. Sin separates us from God and from one another and, yes, we may have differences in theology, liturgy, or polity. But Jesus died on the cross for all, uniting us under the banner of his love. God gathers us into the community of all who believe in Christ and calls us to be saints.

Prayer

God, help us to recognize our common humanity, destiny, and purpose, and to live lives of grace and peace, now and forever. Amen.

February 15

1 Corinthians 1:4-7

I give thanks to my God always for you because of the grace of God that has been given you in Christ Jesus, for in every way you have been enriched in him, in speech and knowledge of every kind—just as the testimony of Christ has been strengthened among you—so that you are not lacking in any spiritual gift as you wait for the revealing of our Lord Jesus Christ.

To ponder

There is no greater gift than realizing the constant presence of the Divine and His Absolute Power to create and restore all things.—Marta Mrotek, *Miracle in Progress*

Celebrating diverse gifts

During the season of Lent, we become aware of the many ways in which we are saturated in the grace of God. We give thanks for this, for we know that apart from God, we can do nothing.

Our continuous prayer is for God to season our speech and to enliven our knowledge so we bear witness to God's love and grace, and our family, friends, and neighbors hear and receive the good news revealed in Christ Jesus. The work of the Holy Spirit in and through us emboldens our testimonies.

The Spirit also blesses us with varying spiritual gifts to build up the church and the world. How boring would our world be if we were all the same? The diversity of our gifts equips the church to share the love of Jesus. Some of us will sing. Others of us will dance. Others will preach, teach, or serve. Some of us will paint and others will recite poetry. Our gifts, as varied as our persons, are all bestowed on us by the grace of God.

Prayer

Holy One, help us not to be jealous of the gifts of others but to enthusiastically celebrate one another as bearers of your love and grace. Amen.

1 Corinthians 1:10-12

Now I appeal to you, brothers and sisters, by the name of our Lord Jesus Christ, that all of you be in agreement and that there be no divisions among you, but that you be united in the same mind and the same purpose. For it has been reported to me by Chloe's people that there are quarrels among you.... What I mean is that each of you says, "I belong to Paul," or "I belong to Apollos," or "I belong to Cephas," or "I belong to Christ."

To ponder

It is not our differences that divide us. It is our inability to recognize, accept, and celebrate those differences.—Audre Lorde, *Sister Outsider*

Walking together

We are all sinners saved by grace, and one of our greatest sins is the inability to see in every human the image and likeness of God.

When Paul wrote to the folks at Corinth, he was disappointed by the fact that they were dividing themselves into camps based on which leader they loved most. In the church today we continue to silo ourselves based on race, gender, class, sexual orientation, political affiliations, and the like. How grievous this must be for Jesus, who died for us all!

Paul reminds us that we are at our best when we walk with one another, unified by our commonalities and celebrating our diversity. As we imbibe the beauty of God's creation, we see diversity everywhere! It is in the colors of the flowers, the neck lengths of various creatures, the size and shape of each life form, and the majesty of the assorted galaxies. God values diversity in all things—including people. So shall we.

Prayer

Gracious God, help us to put away quarreling and to trust in you. Give us a common purpose and empower us to walk together in unity. Amen.

February 17

1 Corinthians 1:17-18

Christ [sent me] to proclaim the gospel, and not with eloquent wisdom, so that the cross of Christ might not be emptied of its power.

For the message about the cross is foolishness to those who are perishing, but to us who are being saved it is the power of God.

To ponder

Mount Calvary is the academy of love.—St. Francis de Sales, "Treatise on the Love of God"

The foolishness and power of the cross

In our contemporary culture, people are admired for having material possessions, money, power, titles, and fame. The message of the cross appears to be foolish and weak in this setting. After all, in the world's eyes Jesus had nothing. How could love alone be enough to save all of creation from perishing? Certainly we could be saved through our own power or might, right? Wrong!

The blessed Lenten season reminds us that we cannot save ourselves. It is not by our own doing that we earn everlasting life. In fact, nothing we do—or don't do—opens wide the gates of heaven. Instead it is the "foolishness" of what Jesus wrought on the cross that saves us. It is love that lifts us. Indeed the cross is the "academy of love" for it shows just how far God is willing to go to forgive and redeem us from our transgressions. In return we love and serve Christ above all others.

Prayer

Thank you, God, that in the cross we experience your power to save. When we could not save ourselves, you saved us! Thank you for your incomprehensible love for all creation. Amen.

1 Corinthians 1:27-31

God chose what is foolish in the world to shame the wise; God chose what is weak in the world to shame the strong; God chose what is low and despised in the world, things that are not, to reduce to nothing things that are, so that no one might boast in the presence of God. He is the source of your life in Christ Jesus, who became for us wisdom from God, and righteousness and sanctification and redemption, in order that, as it is written, "Let the one who boasts, boast in the Lord."

To ponder

Before God, we are all equally wise—and equally foolish.
—Albert Einstein, *Einstein on Cosmic Religion*

Time to slow down

Albert Einstein is arguably one of the smartest humans to ever live upon the earth. Yet even he understood that before God we are all equally wise and foolish. Isn't it amazing that Einstein considered himself equal to all human beings in God's presence? It's true. In comparison to God, our wisdom amounts to nothing.

The apostle Paul writes that God chooses what is foolish, weak, low, and despised so that no one has cause to boast. Perhaps we spend too much of our time and energy trying to earn the accolades of others or to impress people with our wisdom, strength, or power. Could it be that Jesus' sacrifice upon an old, rugged cross frees us to rest instead in God's unconditional, amazing grace?

During this Lenten season, breathe deeply of God's grace and stop striving for fortune, fame, and glory. In Lent, God grants us time to slow down, rest, and meditate on the life and legacy of Jesus, his sacrifice upon the cross, and his triumph over sin, death, and the grave.

Prayer

O God, help us to cease our striving and to hear you declare that we are loved beyond our wildest imagining. Through the cross you have accomplished all that was needed for our salvation. We are forever grateful. Amen.

1 Corinthians 2:1-2, 4-5

When I came to you, brothers and sisters, I did not come proclaiming the mystery of God to you in lofty words or wisdom. For I decided to know nothing among you except Jesus Christ, and him crucified. . . . My speech and my proclamation were not with plausible words of wisdom, but with a demonstration of the Spirit and of power, so that your faith might rest not on human wisdom but on the power of God.

To ponder

When the poor of North America and the Third World read the passion story of the cross, they do not view it as a theological idea but as God's suffering solidarity with the victims of the world.—James Cone, "An African-American Perspective on the Cross and Suffering"

The good news of the cross

Paul announced the great "mystery of God" to the Corinthians. We might imagine this mystery to be the vastness of the universe that God created. Images from the James Webb Space Telescope show us how tiny a place we have in the cosmos.

The people of Corinth were not able to see images from space, but they were surrounded by the might of the Roman Empire. The world beyond them was vast and powerful. They knew they were insignificant in comparison because among the followers of Jesus "not many of [them] were wise by human standards, not many were powerful, not many were of noble birth" (1 Corinthians 1:26). Surely to glimpse the mystery of God meant looking to the world beyond themselves.

Paul, however, proclaimed the mystery that God's power and wisdom could be found in what appeared to be weak and foolish. In the cross, in Christ's suffering and solidarity with the oppressed, the Corinthians found good news.

Prayer

God of surprises, you stand with those ignored, abused, or oppressed by others. In Christ crucified, you hang with other crucified people. Teach us to know and embrace this mystery. Amen.

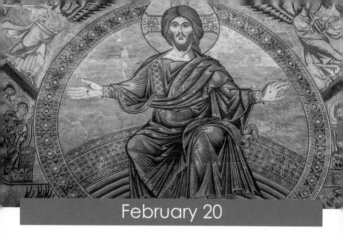

February 20

1 Corinthians 2:7-8

We speak God's wisdom, secret and hidden, which God decreed before the ages for our glory. None of the rulers of this age understood this; for if they had, they would not have crucified the Lord of glory.

To ponder

Faith in the resurrection affirms that God has the last word for this executed victim of state injustice and that word, blessedly, is life.—Elizabeth Johnson, *She Who Is*

The crucified Lord of glory

God sent Jesus to reveal God's glory to us. *Glory*, like the word *mystery*, can carry many meanings.

Jesus did not embody what the world around him thought of as glory—power, profits, prestige, and honor. The rulers of that age rejected the notion that nails and a cross could dispose of anyone who was truly glorious.

But God saw glory in Jesus' partnership with broken people. Jesus glorified God in his compassion for those caught in sin. Though the powerful destroyed Jesus, nailing him to a cross, God raised him up. God's final word about Jesus is "This one got it right! Jesus showed you my way." The one who loved people throughout his life returned to be love for them again. He returns to be love for us again. The glory of God is the embrace shared with a broken people.

Prayer

God of life, in Jesus we see the way you have prepared for us. When the rulers of our age seek to destroy those who are compassionate and merciful, teach us to not fear their threats, but to act with courage. Raise us up to love and to live in the healing way of Jesus. Amen.

February 21

1 Corinthians 2:12-13

Now we have received not the spirit of the world, but the Spirit that is from God, so that we may understand the gifts bestowed on us by God. And we speak of these things in words not taught by human wisdom but taught by the Spirit, interpreting spiritual things to those who are spiritual.

To ponder

We lose faith the moment we lose our capacity for imagination. Without faith, there is no imagination; without imagination, there is no innovation; without innovation, there is no future. Faith embodies the view that we can imagine something that was not, until the present, part of our history.
—Mitri Raheb, *Faith in the Face of Empire*

18

Schooled by the Spirit

The world presses in so hard upon us that sometimes we assume that the suffering of this moment and the structures that create it will endure forever. What Paul calls "the spirit of the world" wants us to lose hope and believe that tomorrow will hold more of the hardship we have known today. In this spirit, nothing will ever change.

God's Spirit is different. The Spirit of God comes into locked-up places to set us free to live in a different kind of wisdom. This wisdom is grounded in the future that God is preparing for us. Taught by God's Spirit, our imaginations are called forth and new life for us as individuals and as a people becomes possible again.

We are called to speak of this hoped-for change. God's gifted future awaits us all. In fact, this future gift becomes our present today. This word from God transforms the world that God loves.

Prayer

Send your Holy Spirit upon us, God, that we might not be overwhelmed or filled with despair, but trust in the future you are preparing. Stir up your power that our sacred imaginations may thrive. We pray in the Spirit of Jesus, who is always calling us forward. Amen.

1 Corinthians 3:1-3

I could not speak to you as spiritual people, but rather as people of the flesh, as infants in Christ. I fed you with milk, not solid food, for you were not ready for solid food. Even now you are still not ready, for you are still of the flesh. For as long as there is jealousy and quarreling among you, are you not of the flesh, and behaving according to human inclinations?

To ponder

Kindness eases change.
Love quiets fear.
—Octavia Butler, *Parable of the Talents*

Not quarreling but kindness

Paul introduced the Corinthians to the gospel of Jesus Christ, but they had to also learn something about God's long commitment to the world witnessed to in what we call the Old Testament. Many did not know the story of how God called Abram and Sarai to leave their home for a new place. They had not heard of how God liberated the people from slavery in Egypt. The prophets' words had neither challenged them nor given them hope. In this sense, they came to the faith as babies needing to learn how to speak. In terms of their discipleship, they were learning to pull themselves up and take their first toddling steps.

What kept the people in Corinth from walking forward was what often keeps us from moving forward. They were worried that some were favored more than others, and fought among themselves. Growth would only happen if they settled into the nourishment that Paul had already provided them. If they understood the mercy shown to them in Christ crucified, they could learn to practice that mercy toward each other.

Change is difficult, but kindness makes it possible. A well-nursed child grows in trust that she will receive good care.

Prayer

Mothering God, you hold us in loving arms and feed us of yourself that we might grow in body and spirit. May we trust your love, knowing that when the time for weaning comes, your care continues in solid ways. Amen.

1 Corinthians 3:5-6

What then is Apollos? What is Paul? Servants through whom you came to believe, as the Lord assigned to each. I planted, Apollos watered, but God gave the growth.

To ponder

Every time I have reached the edge of how far I believed love could go, I have found myself instead standing in the middle of where love has already been.—Emmy Kegler, *One Coin Found*

Growing and going with God

We sometimes use the best gifts in the worst ways. The Corinthians had known some inspirational leaders. Paul was there at the beginning. He came and preached to them God's gift in the crucified Christ. When Paul moved on, Apollos picked up the instruction, giving the Corinthians what they needed so their faith could sprout and stretch toward heaven. But some people replaced the message with the messenger. Paul declares that God—not Paul, not Apollos—undergirds the whole process and is the source of all growth.

Our most gifted leaders are still fallible followers of Jesus. God, however, is faithful in, with, and through our blossoming in the gospel. Precious people in our lives lead us part of the way, but the God of love moves out in front of them, beyond them, that love might take over the whole of the terrain.

What a joy to discover that God's harvest always exceeds our expectations. We fallible followers discover that when we fall short, God's love shows itself greater than our failures. We also know this when we see God's teeming, greening gospel creeping over the fences we have built and finding life in our neighbors' yards.

Prayer

God of the gospel, let us grow with you, anticipating your movement beyond the boundaries we have constructed to hedge you in. Let us follow your love everywhere you take us. Amen.

1 Corinthians 3:10-11

According to the grace of God given to me, like a skilled master builder I laid a foundation, and someone else is building on it. Each builder must choose with care how to build on it. For no one can lay any foundation other than the one that has been laid; that foundation is Jesus Christ.

To ponder

[Eula:] "I don't question God."
[Caroletta:] "But maybe you should question the people who taught you this version of God. Because it's not doing you any favors."—Deesha Philyaw, *The Secret Lives of Church Ladies*

God is as Jesus does

In the conversation above, two women discuss the puny and petty beliefs they've been taught about God. Eula learned a version of God as ever-vigilant, watching to make sure she did not step out of line. This God found it suspect if Eula had joy in her life. The God her teachers described kept Eula in her place, subservient and obedient.

Our understanding of God is the foundation upon which our whole faith is built. The gospel calls us to build our life of faith on the revelation of God in Jesus Christ. If you want to know what God is like, pay attention to Jesus. God is as Jesus does. Jesus opens up to us the heart of God's compassion and love. This God is always ready to offer us an expansive place to dwell. Any God who contradicts this generous and caring God is no God at all. In the life, death, and resurrection of Jesus, we come to understand the steadfast commitment of God to our well-being. This God is not ashamed to do us some favors, for in Christ we are the favored ones of God.

Prayer

Compassionate God, let us abandon all notions of you that are puny and petty. Christ, the one who is so close to your heart, reveals the expansive nature of your love. Draw us into that embrace. Amen.

1 Corinthians 3:21-23

All things are yours, whether Paul or Apollos or Cephas or the world or life or death or the present or the future—all belong to you, and you belong to Christ, and Christ belongs to God.

To ponder

The God, who is greater than God, has only one thing on Her mind, and that is to drop, endlessly, rose petals on our heads. Behold the One who can't take His eyes off of you. Marinate in the vastness of that.—Gregory Boyle, *Tattoos on the Heart*

Extravagant welcome

We all go looking for spaces of belonging. We wander into the high school cafeteria and wonder where to sit. We move to a new town hoping to find "our people." We value the friends who come over for dinner not caring whether the house is a mess. We want places where we are known, appreciated, and loved. We need places that we can return to and find welcome and acceptance.

Paul suggests circles of belonging to illustrate our relationships with God and one another. As with Russian nesting dolls, the largest circle encompasses everything. That largest circle of belonging is God, to whom Christ belongs. As those who belong to Christ, we are held within Christ as he is also held in God. This means all of us live, move, and have our being in this double divine embrace. This belonging to Christ and to God means that we also belong to one another.

Finally, all things that are God's are shared with us: creation, life, beauty, joy, salvation. To assure us of all this, God lavishes attention and care upon us. God is filled with delight to encircle us and all creation with love and grace.

Prayer

God, our home, you have made space for us in your relationship with Christ so that we are encircled by love. Help us to look at one another the way you look upon us. Let us claim and care for all that you have given us as our inheritance. Amen.

February 26

1 Corinthians 4:1

Think of us in this way, as servants of Christ and stewards of God's mysteries.

To ponder

We are quite capable, thus, of living in a world even while it is being reconstructed, and of ourselves participating in the reshaping of our concepts and categories at the very moment we are using them to order our experience and give it meaning.
—Gordon D. Kaufman, *In Face of Mystery*

Stewards of God's mysteries

We might picture stewarding God's mysteries much like financial stewardship. I know what is in my bank account, and I am responsible for figuring out the best way to disperse whatever money I have among the many bills and causes that call out for my attention. At the end of the day, I can record it all on a spreadsheet or use an app to see where things stand. But stewarding the mysteries of God does not work this way.

To steward the mysteries of God is to embrace the lively, living reality of God and the language we use to invoke that reality—and to actively resist every human attempt to tame or contain these mysteries within categories that we find comfortable. To steward divine mysteries is to give our talents, time, and money to God and encourage others to do the same, knowing that it will be impossible to account for all the ways God uses our gifts to bring hope and healing to the neighborhood, the community, and the world.

The Greek word for *mystery* has also been used for the sacraments of baptism and holy communion. As stewards we gratefully receive the sacraments and welcome others into these divine mysteries.

Prayer

Sacred Mystery, be who you are that we might become who we are meant to be. In the name of Jesus, your mystery among us. Amen.

1 Corinthians 4:10-13

We are fools for the sake of Christ, . . . we are hungry and thirsty, we are poorly clothed and beaten and homeless, and we grow weary from the work of our own hands. When reviled, we bless; when persecuted, we endure; when slandered, we speak kindly.

To ponder

This is obvious: if anyone's foot hurts, yes, even the little toe, the eye at once looks at it, the fingers grasp it, the face puckers, the whole body bends over it, and all are concerned with this small member; again, once it is cared for, all the other members are benefited.—Martin Luther, "The Blessed Sacrament of the Holy and True Body of Christ"

Suffering in solidarity

The apostle Paul's theology of the body of Christ not only mentioned feet, it was involved in every step of his ministry. Because he believed that those who belonged to Christ were one body, Paul committed himself to leave behind his own privileges to stand with those who knew hunger and thirst as constant companions. In this way he became a "fool" for Christ.

Just as a rock dropped upon the toe instantly invites every other part of the body to rush to the aid of the injured party, the suffering of other people drew all of Paul's energy and attention. His commitment to Christ was so strong that, in the end, the plight of those who were suffering became fully his own. In shared suffering with those deep in the shadow of death, he gained credibility to announce the "foolishness" that God's power is known in weakness.

This solidarity in suffering was modeled on the ministry of the crucified Christ, which shaped Paul in another way. When he faced hostility, he responded with kindness. Like Jesus pardoning those who crucified him, Paul understood that his enemies were included in God's mercy.

Prayer

Holy God, you show mercy to those who do not know the way of mercy. May we do the same. In Jesus' merciful name we pray. Amen.

February 28

1 Corinthians 4:15-17

In Christ Jesus I became your father through the gospel. I
appeal to you, then, be imitators of me. For this reason I sent
you Timothy, who is my beloved and faithful child in the Lord,
to remind you of my ways in Christ Jesus, as I teach them
everywhere in every church.

To ponder

Blood does not family make. Those are relatives. Family are
those with whom you share your good, bad, and ugly, and still
love one another in the end. These are the ones you select.
—Hector Xtravaganza, in "A Glittering Goodbye to Hector
Xtravaganza"

Family matters

Paul refers to himself as "father through the gospel" to the Corinthians and to Timothy. This may seem strange to us, but Paul's letters are full of him establishing new, non-biological familial relationships, which some call "chosen family" today. From the cross Jesus too established a new relationship between his mother, Mary, and his disciple, John (John 19:26-27), ensuring that both would be cared for after his death.

Paul understands that bonds of love and faithfulness are not limited to biological family, and they have the power to turn the world on its head, to set the suffering free from the chains of injustice. He ensures that, whatever their biological families of origin might say or do, the early followers of Jesus know they have soft places to land where they will be welcomed, loved, and treated like kinfolk in God's family.

Today chosen families continue to provide soft places to land, with people to whom God has bonded us, and through whose love God is made flesh. Chosen families are especially important to LGBTQIA+ people and others who have experienced disrespect, derision, or rejection from their biological families or the church.

Prayer

God, our Holy Relative, provide everyone with soft places to land where they are treated with love and respect. Move us and the church to welcome, love, and treasure all people as kinfolk in your family. Amen.

February 29

1 Corinthians 6:19-20

Do you not know that your body is a temple of the Holy
Spirit within you, which you have from God, and that you are
not your own? For you were bought with a price; therefore
glorify God in your body.

To ponder

A baby is God's opinion that life should go on.—Carl
Sandburg, *Remembrance Rock*

Glorifying God

Today's scripture text from 1 Corinthians closes the section
on sexual immorality. There has been much debate in recent
decades regarding the exact types of sexual immorality Paul

refers to here, but what is clear is that this issue involves oppression and profound imbalances of power.

When we consider our bodies as temples where God's Spirit dwells, the idea of using them to oppress others becomes anathema. If my body and your body are both homes of the Divine, we are called to treat them with gentleness and care. Take a moment to ponder how you might prepare a room for the arrival of the Christ-child. How would you go about making the room safe, filling it with good things, curating a space that speaks of your love?

Often people deprive their bodies of things they enjoy by "giving up" something for Lent. While it is possible that, say, eating chocolate creates a barrier between us and God, giving up chocolate for a season most likely focuses our attention on what *we* are doing. As we journey through Lent this year, let's consider what *God* is doing. Our bodies are temples where the Holy encounters us and sets us free.

Prayer

God of love, we live in you and you in us. Thank you for the gift of this love. Help us to look upon our bodies and those of others secure in the knowledge that we are looking at you. Amen.

March 1

1 Corinthians 7:17

Let each of you lead the life that the Lord has assigned, to which God called you.

To ponder

Remembering that you are going to die is the best way I know to avoid the trap of thinking you have something to lose.
—Steve Jobs, commencement address, Stanford University

Navigating life

First Corinthians 7:17 has been used for much of Christian history to convince people to endure suffering—instructing the poor not to object when the rich refuse to share, encouraging people who are sick or living with disabilities to endure terrible pain, even urging people to stay with abusive spouses. But these interpretations completely ignore the context in which the verse was written.

Paul, and in turn, those in the communities he founded, believed that Christ's return was imminent. Paul instructs people to not spend the last days hustling to seek earthly accomplishments, but rather to be who they are, where they are, and to focus on preparing for what life will be like when all the promises of God are fully realized.

We know that Christ did not bodily return during Paul's lifetime. We lead a much more liminal existence. We must live as though Christ is returning tomorrow, while at the same time living as though his return might happen in a hundred, or a thousand, or a billion tomorrows. Figuring out how to navigate life oriented both to the present and the future isn't easy, but it can be holy. The question before us is not just "How would you live if you knew that God's promises would come true tomorrow?" but "How are you going to live, knowing that God's promises are coming true every day—some of them through you?"

Prayer

Holy God, we give you thanks for the gift of your coming in Christ. Bless us as we seek to orient ourselves toward your eternal presence. Amen.

1 Corinthians 8:5-6

Even though there may be so-called gods in heaven or on earth . . . for us there is one God, the Father, from whom are all things and for whom we exist, and one Lord, Jesus Christ, through whom are all things and through whom we exist.

To ponder

I take you, [name], to be my [spouse],
to join with you and share all that is to come,
and I promise to be faithful to you until death parts us.
—*ELW*

An unbreakable bond

People new to the Bible are often surprised to find that it mentions other "so-called" deities besides the God of Sarah and Abraham, Miriam and Moses, Mary and Joseph. It simply remarks that *this* is the God with whom we (practitioners of Abrahamic faiths) have an unbreakable bond, the one who has claimed us and to whom we have devoted ourselves.

Because of this, marriage metaphors abound in scripture. They illustrate the relationship between humans and this God who creates, sustains, and saves us. References to the marriage rite, while still abundant in Jewish worship practice, have largely fallen out of favor in Christian worship, but the burning passion and dogged devotion with which God's love pursues us never fades.

The holy One, who continually chooses you, asks you to forsake all others and devote yourself anew each day to this relationship. What commitments, promises, freedoms, and celebrations will you observe as you live in this unbreakable bond?

Prayer

Passionate God, we are yours and you are ours. You have captured our hearts and we devote ourselves to you. Forgive us when we stray and draw us back into your loving arms. Amen.

March 3 / Lent 3

1 Corinthians 9:22-23

I have become all things to all people, that I might by all means save some. I do it all for the sake of the gospel, so that I may share in its blessings.

To ponder

It is our duty to fight for our freedom.
It is our duty to win.
We must love each other and support each other.
We have nothing to lose but our chains.
—Assata Shakur, "To My People"

For the gospel's sake

Paul's life—his teaching, preaching, traveling, writing, and imprisonment—could be summed up in the words, "I do it all for the sake of the gospel." His passion for evangelism, bringing the gospel message to others, was behind everything he did and said.

The Protestant movement began with rabble-rousers taking the pope and others to task for abandoning their gospel call. But generally speaking, mainline Protestants, including Lutherans, are no longer known for our burning desire to share the gospel with those in power and with those who have been wounded by the powers that be.

This is essential work, but it is not easy. It requires that we show up in places that make us uncomfortable and come alongside people who have less power than we do. At times it may require that we preach not to people in need, but to those oppressing them. Most of all, it requires that we become not what we *assume* vulnerable populations need, but what they *actually* need. This means confessing, repenting, and changing course—over and over again.

Prayer

God of connection, thank you for your word. Bless us as we seek to listen to one another and to share the gospel with others. Amen.

1 Corinthians 12:4-6

Now there are varieties of gifts, but the same Spirit; and there are varieties of services, but the same Lord; and there are varieties of activities, but it is the same God who activates all of them in everyone.

To ponder

I know I'm somebody, 'cause God made me, and God don't make no junk!—Ethel Waters, in *His Eye Is on the Sparrow*

Made in God's image

Ethel Waters was a legend of stage, screen, recording studio, and—late in her life—of the preaching circuit. She was a world-renowned singer who then turned her sights on the acting world, becoming the first Black American to land the leading role in a television show, and in 1962 the first Black American to win a Primetime Emmy. But she was more than that. She was Black, and a woman, and disabled, and bisexual, at a time when all those things were treated as less than human. She was born to a teenage mother who had been raped, and was married off to a violent husband when she was thirteen years old. In the eyes of the world, she was worth less than nothing. That's what she too believed about herself, for much of her life. But eventually she came to faith in Christ, and in doing so realized that being made in God's image meant she was worthy. Worthy of love, respect, and kindness. Worthy to share her story and God's story with others who might benefit.

Who in your orbit might feel as though they are worth less than nothing? Who might not see their God-given gifts because the world doesn't see them? And how might you let these people know that they are seen, heard, gifted, needed, valued, and loved?

Prayer

You have searched me, O Lord, and you know me. Help me to see and encourage the gifts of others, so that they know they are fearfully and wonderfully made, joining us together in love and service. Amen.

1 Corinthians 12:7-11

To each is given the manifestation of the Spirit for the common good. To one is given through the Spirit the utterance of wisdom, and to another the utterance of knowledge according to the same Spirit, to another faith by the same Spirit, to another gifts of healing by the one Spirit, to another the working of miracles, to another prophecy, to another the discernment of spirits, to another various kinds of tongues, to another the interpretation of tongues. All these are activated by one and the same Spirit.

To ponder

Equipped by prayer, we live the Spirit's call.
Empower'd to serve with gifts, both great and small,

we bring the living hope of God to all.
Alleluia!
—ACS 1048

For the good of all

God has given you your life, your body, and your gifts. Paul gives several examples of gifts in today's scripture text: wisdom, knowledge, faith, healing, miracles, prophecy, discernment, tongues, and interpretation. This list is by no means exhaustive! Paul mentions some of these gifts, but also a few more in Romans 12:6-7: ministry, teaching, encouragement, generosity, leadership, and compassion. And Paul describes even more gifts as "fruits" of the Spirit—"love, joy, peace, patience, kindness, generosity, faithfulness, gentleness, and self-control" (Galatians 5:22-23).

What are your gifts? You and I don't have the same gifts, but the same Spirit gives us our unique gifts and sets them in motion for the good of all creation.

How might the Spirit be calling you to use your gifts?

Prayer

Gracious God, we give you thanks for pouring out gifts on us for the common good. Give us grace to discern those gifts and to use them in serving others, that we and the world might be healed. Amen.

March 6

1 Corinthians 12:12-13

Just as the body is one and has many members, and all the members of the body, though many, are one body, so it is with Christ. For in the one Spirit we were all baptized into one body—Jews or Greeks, slaves or free—and we were all made to drink of one Spirit.

To ponder

Now with praise and thanksgiving, we join the song.
All are welcome! We gather to sing loud and strong.
Not enslaved, but set free! From now on, all will be
One in Jesus, one in water, baptized and set free!
—ELW 453

One

Baptism is no mere ritual for Paul. It is radical transformation—a new way of seeing and being. We are baptized into Christ's death. Buried with Christ, we die to ourselves and rise from the waters of baptism to a new life. We are now Christ's body in the world, made one in Jesus by the one Spirit in one baptism. We are set free to serve God and others.

Emerging from the waters of baptism, we become part of a new humanity. Paul sees all people worshiping together as one, people of all ethnicities, backgrounds, and social classes sharing of their food and their lives. Paul doesn't deny that there are people enslaved by others at that time; he simply deconstructs it as much as he can from his limited perspective. In another letter, he expands on our unity in Christ: "There is no longer Jew or Greek; there is no longer slave or free; there is no longer male and female, for all of you are one in Christ Jesus" (Galatians 3:28).

Paul calls the Corinthians to be the church, one body united by one Spirit. How are we the church in the world today?

Prayer

Gracious God, thank you for setting us all free and making us one through baptism. Empower us by your Spirit to be the body of Christ in the world. Amen.

1 Corinthians 12:14-15, 18

The body does not consist of one member but of many. If the foot would say, "Because I am not a hand, I do not belong to the body," that would not make it any less a part of the body.... But as it is, God arranged the members in the body, each one of them, as he chose.

To ponder

This is Christ's body, broken and blest.
Feed us with mercy and love.
We are Christ's body, broken and blest.
Heal us and make us one.
—ACS 967

Unity in diversity

Our bodies are incredible. Your heart beats and your lungs breathe your entire life, without you consciously thinking about it. Eyes are masterful instruments that refract light. Many people blink every three to five seconds. The tongue has 8,000 tastebuds. You have 100,000 miles of blood vessels. Everything works together to make possible all the things you do.

Paul pictures the church as a body, the body of Christ. When the church functions as it is meant to do, the many parts do not try to one-up or criticize each other. The foot doesn't see itself as less important than the hand. The church needs all the parts to contribute their gifts and work together as one.

What would happen if all the hands went to one church and all the feet went to another? Ditto eyes and ears. In a polarized society, we are at risk of that today. The problem Paul sees in Corinth is still with us.

God creates a kaleidoscope of people and gifts. Our differences are a strength, not a weakness, when we listen to one another and learn how to work together.

Prayer

We give you thanks, O God, for the great diversity in the world. Help us to love all the people you place in our path, and teach us to work together, as the body of Christ. Amen.

March 8

1 Corinthians 12:24-26

God has so arranged the body . . . that there may be no dissension within the body, but the members may have the same care for one another. If one member suffers, all suffer together with it; if one member is honored, all rejoice together with it.

To ponder

We share our mutual woes,
our mutual burdens bear,
and often for each other flows
the sympathizing tear.
—ELW 656

All suffer together

Her husband died at home on a fall morning. The neighbors were there when the pastor arrived. Then some church members came by, then more, and more. Some brought food. Some talked. Others just sat quietly and wept with her. Eventually, out-of-town family showed up and the first wave of visitors gave the family space to grieve and begin thinking about arrangements.

This is the body of Christ. It is bigger than the local congregation. It is the great cloud of witnesses that come, sit, and listen. "God has so arranged the body," Paul says. Indeed. It is often this care for one another that helps us through those times when dissension arises.

Let us be the body of Christ by treating one another with respect and honor: "Let love be genuine; hate what is evil, hold fast to what is good; love one another with mutual affection; outdo one another in showing honor. . . . Rejoice with those who rejoice, weep with those who weep" (Romans 12:9-10, 15).

Prayer

Gracious God, draw us in the Spirit's tether, for we know that whenever two or three are gathered in Jesus' name, you are there. May mutual love and friendship abound, so the body of Christ is strengthened for ministry in Jesus' name. Amen.

1 Corinthians 12:27-31

Now you are the body of Christ and individually members of it. And God has appointed in the church first apostles, second prophets, third teachers; then deeds of power, then gifts of healing, forms of assistance, forms of leadership, various kinds of tongues. Are all apostles? Are all prophets? Are all teachers? Do all work miracles? Do all possess gifts of healing? Do all speak in tongues? Do all interpret? But strive for the greater gifts. And I will show you a still more excellent way.

To ponder

The place God calls you to is the place where your deep gladness and the world's deep hunger meet.—Frederick Buechner, *Wishful Thinking*

Gifts to serve

The gifts from the Spirit are countless! In today's scripture text, Paul adds prophets, teachers, healers, assistants, leaders, and more to earlier lists. We might add pastors, musicians, accountants, maintenance workers, home builders, hospital visitors, prison chaplains, refugee resettlers, meal servers, and more. Think of all the gifts that it takes to be the church in your faith community, the neighborhood, and the world.

One person's job drives another person to distraction. Some find keeping financial books a struggle. Others find hospital visitation difficult. Some are phenomenal cooks, while others excel with technology. Thank goodness we are not all the same.

Paul asks seven consecutive rhetorical questions. Are all apostles? (No, not everyone is cut out for it.) Are all prophets? (Heavens, no! We know what happens to prophets.) Are all teachers? (Of course not.) And on Paul goes.

You are good at something, probably several things. Your call lies at the intersection of your gifts and the world's need. God has given you these gifts and passions to serve the world. This takes a village, so thank God that we're not all the same.

Prayer

Giver of all good gifts, thank you for the amazing diversity of gifts among all people. Help us to discern where our gifts meet the world's greatest need. Amen.

March 10 / Lent 4

1 Corinthians 13:1-3

If I speak in the tongues of mortals and of angels, but do not have love, I am a noisy gong or a clanging cymbal. And if I have prophetic powers, and understand all mysteries and all knowledge, and if I have all faith, so as to remove mountains, but do not have love, I am nothing. If I give away all my possessions, and if I hand over my body so that I may boast, but do not have love, I gain nothing.

To ponder

God is love, and [those] who dwell in love dwell in God, and God in [them].—Meister Eckhart, Sermon 5

God so loved

First Corinthians 13 is often read at Christian weddings, but it's not about marriage. Paul is talking about life. After speaking about a wide variety of gifts, Paul wants the Corinthian church to know that these gifts are worthless unless enveloped in love. We may speak eloquently, have prophetic powers, or have superior knowledge and wisdom, but without love, we are just making noise. We may be incredibly generous or even pay the ultimate sacrifice by giving away our lives, but if we do so without love, we have gained nothing. Even incredible faith is nothing without love. Those are astounding words coming from Paul, who taught that we are saved by grace through faith.

Superior speech, prophecy, knowledge, wisdom, faith, generosity, and sacrifice are all valuable gifts, but on their own they mean nothing. It is love, God's love in us, that energizes them and activates them for the good of all creation.

Prayer

Gracious God, teach us today to love as you so loved the world that you sent your Son, Jesus Christ our Lord. Amen.

March 11

1 Corinthians 13:4-8

Love is patient; love is kind; love is not envious or boastful or arrogant or rude. It does not insist on its own way; it is not irritable or resentful; it does not rejoice in wrongdoing, but rejoices in the truth. It bears all things, believes all things, hopes all things, endures all things. Love never ends.

To ponder

Darkness cannot drive out darkness; only light can do that. Hate cannot drive out hate, only love can do that.
—Martin Luther King Jr., *Strength to Love*

Love is as love does

We use the word *love* in a lot of ways. We fall in love. We say we love pizza or chocolate. We make commitments to another person, to family, to friends out of love. Is love a sentimental, warm feeling, or is there more to it? What does God's love look and feel like? How does it play out in everyday life?

Paul describes love as the presence of patience and kindness. Love is the absence of envy, boasting, arrogance, rudeness, irritability, and resentment. Love gracefully bends a bit, rather than demanding that everything be done its way. It celebrates truth, not wrongdoing. It bears, believes, hopes, and endures all things. Finally, love never ends. It lasts forever.

This is a very high bar. Someone once said, "Your actions are so loud, I can't hear what you're saying." So, what *is* love? Love is God's love in us, turned inside out. It emanates from us in commitment and action. It is so central to our spiritual lives that Jesus said, "By this everyone will know that you are my disciples, if you have love for one another" (John 13:35).

Prayer

Thanks be to you, Lord Jesus Christ, most merciful redeemer, for the countless blessings and benefits you give. May we know you more clearly, love you more dearly, and follow you more nearly, day by day praising you, with the Father and the Holy Spirit, one God, now and forever. Amen. (*ELW*, p. 13)

March 12

1 Corinthians 13:12-13

Now we see in a mirror, dimly, but then we will see face to face. Now I know only in part; then I will know fully, even as I have been fully known. And now faith, hope, and love abide, these three; and the greatest of these is love.

To ponder

Love is not love
Which alters when it alteration finds,
Or bends with the remover to remove.
O no! it is an ever-fixed mark
That looks on tempests and is never shaken.
—Shakespeare, Sonnet 116

Eternal love

Is there a more eloquent treatise on love than 1 Corinthians 13? Shakespeare's 116th sonnet comes close, though his focus is more on romantic love. For both Paul and Shakespeare, love endures. It is an "ever-fixed mark." We are tapping into something transcendent here. This is what makes life worth living.

When one is in love, it is hard to contain. It overflows and pours out on everything: every sunset, every person, every meal, every act of kindness. Even enemies are viewed with compassion.

When our bodies return to the dust, when all is said and done, only three things in life will have enduring value: faith, hope, and love. The greatest of these is love, according to Paul. The greatest example of this love is Christ, "who loved us and gave himself up for us" (Ephesians 5:2).

Love is a powerful force that changes hearts and lives. We are claimed by the love of God in Christ, filled with the gift-giving Spirit, and blessed to live in this love.

Prayer

Almighty and ever-living God, increase in us the gifts of faith, hope, and love; that we may love what you love, serving our neighbor with joy, through your Son, Jesus Christ, our Savior and Lord. Amen. (*ELW*, p. 15)

March 13

1 Corinthians 14:26

When you come together, each one has a hymn, a lesson, a revelation, a tongue, or an interpretation. Let all things be done for building up.

To ponder

There is blessing to be found in rhythm and routine. Jesus certainly had plenty of days that weren't recorded in scripture, even as he was contending with the powers of the world.
—Sarah S. Scherschligt, *God Holds You*

From Lent to Lent again

Our shared worship rhythm did not come out of thin air. Bit by bit, year by year, our faith parents strung together traditions, habits, and liturgies into a necklace of community. We sing together, read scripture together, hear preaching and encouragement together, as God's people have done for thousands of years.

When I was younger, some parts of worship felt long. And yet, I kept coming, drawn into the reassuring repetition of worship, the church year, and the lectionary cycle. The rhythms of faith anchored me in ways that the frantic pace of the school year did not.

Every week, we are gathered, fed, and sent. Every year we travel with Jesus through birth, wilderness, teaching, feeding, death, burial, new life, birthing the church, and more. Every three years we make a circuit through the gospels of Matthew, Mark, and Luke (with John sprinkled in). Christ has died, Christ is risen, Christ will come again. Lent will end, and Lent will be here again. During Lent we live inside the story as we gather together, sing hymns together, pray together, sit in silence together, and wait together in hope for that coming dawn to shine on us.

Prayer

God, as we rise, as we serve, and as we rest, sustain us through your son Jesus Christ. Amen.

March 14

1 Corinthians 15:1-2

Now I would remind you, brothers and sisters, of the good news that I proclaimed to you, which you in turn received, in which also you stand, through which also you are being saved, if you hold firmly to the message that I proclaimed to you.

To ponder

The spaces between what was firm and sure are scary unless there is something else to fill them in, something that tells the truth with love.—Meta Herrick Carlson, *Ordinary Blessings for Parents*

Shaking hands, firm grip

"I baptize you in the name of the Father. . . ." Pastor Tony poured water over our daughter's head. She looked puzzled, but she didn't make a peep as her daddy held her firmly over the font. Pastor Tony, who is the other pastor at the church I serve, later told me he was both excited and nervous. Though he has baptized many children over the years, our daughter was his first "pastor's kid"! His hands shook just enough, causing him to drop the oil stock when it came time to anoint her with the sign of the cross. But his hands held firm as he carried her around the sanctuary while the entire congregation welcomed her, their newest sibling in Christ.

Months before this baptism, Pastor Tony's daughter was confirmed. He spoke the words, "Stir up your Holy Spirit . . ." over her head, and I joined her siblings during the laying on of hands—sturdy hands holding her in love and prayer.

Together we stand firm for one another, even when our hands shake, knowing that we are supported by our siblings in Christ in bearing God's message of love to the world, and showing that love to one another.

Prayer

Hold us firmly in your arms, Mighty God, as we go out to serve this world, called and claimed by you. Amen.

March 15

1 Corinthians 15:3-5

I handed on to you as of first importance what I in turn had received: that Christ died for our sins in accordance with the scriptures, and that he was buried, and that he was raised on the third day in accordance with the scriptures, and that he appeared to Cephas, then to the twelve.

To ponder

To be grown, fed, delivered—God put faith in a body.—Cole Arthur Riley, *This Here Flesh*

The cross way

Jesus didn't come to be a great king of history. He wasn't born to be prince over an earthly realm. He wasn't born to be great: he was born to be good. He was born, he lived, and he died to show that the goodness of God is for all people—not just the rich, not just the righteous, not just the powerful. Jesus chose what was good for the entire world, even though it led to his death.

With Jesus, the symbol of an instrument of torture and humiliation and death is transformed. The cross becomes a symbol of life and is repurposed as the way God wants to be known in the world. It is transformed into a sign of divine love that holds nothing back. Jesus received the worst that we had to offer: our selfishness, our fear, the broken mess we've made of our lives. Jesus transforms that too into something beautiful and precious for us to hand off to future generations—we are chosen, beloved children of God.

Prayer

Jesus, help us to see where you are transforming evil into good, and to hand off that good news to others. Amen.

March 16

1 Corinthians 15:6-7

Then he appeared to more than five hundred brothers and sisters at one time, most of whom are still alive, though some have died. Then he appeared to James, then to all the apostles.

To ponder

But if the world is watching, we might as well tell the truth.... The church offers the messy, inconvenient, gut-wrenching, never-ending work of healing and reconciliation.—Rachel Held Evans, *Searching for Sunday*

Then Jesus appeared to YOU

In TV courtroom dramas and true crime podcasts, witnesses are often required to report what they have seen to build a case. When a witness is not cooperating or does something unexpected, lawyers may ask the judge in a very serious tone: "Your honor, permission to treat the witness as hostile." Once that happens, they are not always kind in getting to the truth.

The first disciples shared what they had seen of Jesus. In turn, we, as Jesus' followers, have seen Jesus at work in our lives and in the lives of others, and have become his witnesses in all that we say and do. This is a daunting task. Intentionally or unintentionally, I feel I'm more like a "hostile witness"—clamming up when I should be telling about how God has been at work in my life.

Fortunately for us, Jesus will never treat us as hostile witnesses, even when we fall down on our discipleship jobs of sharing the good news. We are not the last people to see Jesus and his love, just as these five hundred (plus James), plus all the apostles, were not the last people who ever saw Jesus. Jesus is still showing up, changing lives, and calling us to follow him.

Prayer

Give us the passion, words, and wisdom to share where we have experienced your love, gracious Lord. Amen.

March 17 / Lent 5

1 Corinthians 15:8-9

Last of all, as to one untimely born, he appeared also to me.
For I am the least of the apostles, unfit to be called an apostle,
because I persecuted the church of God.

To ponder

Nothing human beings do is set in stone—and even stone
changes, anyway. . . . People who say change is impossible
are usually pretty happy with things just as they are.—N. K.
Jemisin, *The City We Became*

Last to the party

As Paul is writing this letter to the people of Corinth, I wonder if he feels late to a party that is already in full swing. Paul, once called Saul, opens the door to the early Christian community and, like a 1980s movie prom scene, the music grinds to an abrupt halt and everyone stops dancing to stare at him. For a moment, Paul wonders whether they will accept him or kick him out. After all, Paul was well known for his terrible actions to them in the past—behavior much worse than being a class bully. Will they accept that he has turned over a new leaf and wants to join in?

We know what happens to Paul: he was invited in, and he became just as zealous for the Lord as he had been in persecuting followers of Christ. Paul made it his life's mission to invite others to the party too. In fact, we are currently reading his mail, and we have Paul to thank for much of the New Testament. This party is still going (yes, even though it's Lent!) and you're invited. You belong here, so come on in and join the dance.

Prayer

God of new beginnings, inspire us to welcome and embrace the last and the least around us. Amen.

March 18

1 Corinthians 15:10-11

But by the grace of God I am what I am, and his grace toward me has not been in vain. On the contrary, I worked harder than any of them—though it was not I, but the grace of God that is with me.

To ponder

With each step, I'm recognizing barriers built through my rote habits and unrealized prejudice. . . . I must acknowledge compromises that drew me further away from my own soul and your calling. But I'm coming home.—Arianne Braithwaite Lehn, *Ash and Starlight*

Grace on our résumé

Paul writes more in other letters to describe his impressive credentials. He has a résumé that would be the envy of any "LinkedIn" profile. From an impeccable parentage, he rose among the ranks in prestige and influence. In fact, he persecuted early Christians so voraciously that his former name—Saul—struck fear among Jesus' followers.

But then, something unexpected happened. Jesus called Saul, now called Paul, to do a complete 180 and follow Jesus instead. So Paul renounced anything—even his name—if it got in the way of following the call of Jesus. Paul tore down his diplomas and flushed them down the toilet (metaphorically), then threw all his plaques and trophies in the garbage. The only thing that matters on his résumé—and ours—is that our righteousness comes from *God*, not from anything that we do or accomplish. Like Paul, we are created beloved, saved from our broken state, and given a home in the grace of God.

Prayer

Quiet our hustle and still our frantic habits, Lord of all stillness and grace. Amen.

March 19

1 Corinthians 15:12-14

Now if Christ is proclaimed as raised from the dead, how can some of you say there is no resurrection of the dead? If there is no resurrection of the dead, then Christ has not been raised; and if Christ has not been raised, then our proclamation has been in vain and your faith has been in vain.

To ponder

Breathe life into dry bones, so we may know what it is to create. Beckon us to lie down so we may know what it is to rest.—Kayla Craig, *To Light Their Way*

The length of Lent

Winter in northern climates can leave us feeling . . . tired. Tired of shoveling snow off cars and off driveways, tired of the cold and wet weather, tired of the bare trees and gray skies, tired of school closures and canceled meetings. Lent can leave us tired too—worn out by additional worship services or Lenten series and devotionals (even this one!), missing the coffee or another treat we chose to give up. Does it really make a difference? Is all this effort in vain? Will we ever make it to Easter?

The end of the story is hard to imagine while we are still in the middle. The finish line is hidden right now, but it's still there. Spring feels like it will never come, but it always does. When we look back to see how far we've come, we are pleasantly surprised. We will make it through this Lent, just as we did last year's Lent: surrounded by everyone who has helped us along the way—holding us, breathing life into us, just as Jesus does.

Prayer

Loving God, we are weary and weighed down by brokenness and hopelessness, and we lay our burdens at the foot of the cross. Amen.

March 20

1 Corinthians 15:20-22

But in fact Christ has been raised from the dead, the first fruits of those who have died. For since death came through a human being, the resurrection of the dead has also come through a human being; for as all die in Adam, so all will be made alive in Christ.

To ponder

"You won't be absolved of your sins on a dusty road," she said, yet, even as she spoke she knew that although absolution was not to be found so simply, God might be glimpsed there.
—Silvia Moreno-Garcia, *The Daughter of Doctor Moreau*

Sharing faces

Babies love faces: they often respond to seeing them from a very young age. When my daughter was still a baby, I held her on my lap during a Zoom webinar. I was astonished at how much she watched and smiled at the person talking on the screen, while the presenter had no idea she had such an ardent admirer. It didn't matter whether my daughter was watching Zoom meetings or having FaceTime phone conversations with far-away family. She smiled and laughed and reached for the screen—more quickly for people she knew, but every face got a reaction.

She doesn't know yet that while some faces are kind, not all faces she will see out in the world will have her best interests at heart. She hasn't yet learned that people are complex and make mistakes, and that knowledge may someday give her pain. But she will also learn that God loved us so much that God showed us God's face in Jesus, who faced all our pain and complexities head on. She will learn that Jesus smiles on her with that love, and hopefully that too will make her laugh with joy.

Prayer

Thank you, Lord, for revealing your love in the face of your Son, Jesus. In his victory over death, bring us to new life. Amen.

March 21

1 Corinthians 15:47-49

The first man was from the earth, a man of dust; the second
man is from heaven. As was the man of dust, so are those who
are of the dust; and as is the man of heaven, so are those who
are of heaven. Just as we have borne the image of the man of
dust, we will also bear the image of the man of heaven.

To ponder

We are showered every day in gifts, but they are not meant
for us to keep. Their life is in their movement, in inhale and
exhale of our shared breath.—Robin Wall Kimmerer, *Braiding
Sweetgrass*

Painted with dust and destiny

While watching episodes of the BBC's "Portrait Artist of the Year," I'm learning how a portrait can be "an honest bit of painting," can look "yummy," or lack a good "likeness." Before the surprise "sitter" (the person being painted) is revealed, nearly every artist describes their ideal face: they love to paint wrinkles, interesting noses, asymmetric features, weathered skin—the exact opposite of what the world would describe as ideal or beautiful. The winners of each episode are never the portraits that capture the best likeness. The portraits that win are the ones that best capture the light, creatively play around with color, or capture the life and spirit of a person in just a few bold, though incomplete, brushstrokes.

Each of us was created with the likeness of God, bearing the cross of Jesus on our foreheads at baptism. When we fail to acknowledge that likeness in others, we forget our shared humanity. Though the portraits of our lives are not yet finished, our work as likeness-bearers of God is to paint the world with the bold brushstrokes of love, forgiveness, and justice.

Prayer

Imprint your love on our hearts, dear Jesus, that we may see your likeness in all people. Amen.

March 22

1 Corinthians 15:51–52

Listen, I will tell you a mystery! We will not all die, but we will all be changed, in a moment, in the twinkling of an eye, at the last trumpet. For the trumpet will sound, and the dead will be raised imperishable, and we will be changed.

To ponder

This is the resurrection! It is the announcement that life cannot ultimately be conquered by death, that there is no road that is at last swallowed up in an ultimate darkness, that there is strength added when the labors increase, that multiplied peace matches multiplied trials, that life is bottomed by the glad surprise.—Howard Thurman, *Meditations of the Heart*

Mystery

As a Bible scholar, I lead conversations on scripture texts about resurrection. In class settings, people ask logistical questions: When is the "last trumpet"? What about the dead in the meantime? Do they sit around waiting? Do they go immediately to God with Christ? . . . These are natural questions. And our answers, for now, are only working answers.

As a pastor, I have also stood at many gravesides. In these settings, texts like today's sound different. At a graveside, words about resurrection are not theoretical. They speak to our souls. Further, logistical questions become less important. More important is the promise that "we will be changed." This is what Howard Thurman calls "the glad surprise."

In the end, Paul chalks up the logistics to mystery. He uses this word for things revealed by God that are otherwise inaccessible to us (1 Corinthians 2:1; 4:1; 13:2; 14:2). In other words, Paul cannot answer all our questions. He offers only what we need: by God's grace in Christ, we will be changed— made imperishable. And that is enough for us.

Prayer

O God, help us to rest content with the things we do not understand, knowing that, by your mercy in Christ Jesus and the power of the Holy Spirit, all indeed shall be well. Amen.

March 23

1 Corinthians 15:58

My beloved, be steadfast, immovable, always excelling in the work of the Lord, because you know that in the Lord your labor is not in vain.

To ponder

Faith, for me, isn't an argument, a catechism, a philosophical "proof." It is instead a lens, a way of experiencing life, and a willingness to act.—Sara Miles, *Take This Bread*

Persisting in faith

Paul's word of encouragement in 1 Corinthians 15:58 is more specific than it may seem. As the close to the chapter, it urges a community to hold fast to the promise of resurrection—

despite skeptics in the company (verse 12). Paul's closing encouragement forms a bookend to the chapter's beginning, where he raised the idea "unless you have come to believe *in vain*" (verse 2, emphasis added). Now, at the chapter's close, he makes the language more certain: "in the Lord your labor is *not in vain*" (emphasis added). In this setting, "labor" refers primarily to persisting in faith, which will by no means be in vain.

Persisting in faith is not easy. Many things in our daily lives discourage it: societal stereotypes, depersonalizing systems, hostile environments, mean-spirited people, and suffocating obligations. These things make it difficult to excel in faith. It is often far easier to become cynical and jaded.

But Paul reminds us: in the Lord Jesus, no faithful act is in vain. Christ sees your faith. Christ sees your dogged persistence. Christ sees your struggles to keep on keeping on. And Christ assures you that none of it is in vain. However imperfect your faith, Christ sees it, honors it, and stands alongside you to help you excel in it.

Prayer

O Lord, support us all the day long of this troubled life, until the shadows lengthen and the evening comes and the busy world is hushed, the fever of life is over, and our work is done. Then, in your mercy, grant us a safe lodging, and a holy rest, and peace at the last, through Jesus Christ our Lord. Amen. (*ELW*, p. 284)

1 Corinthians 16:13–14

Keep alert, stand firm in your faith, be courageous, be strong. Let all that you do be done in love.

To ponder

The world is indeed full of peril, and in it there are many dark places; but still there is much that is fair, and though in all lands love is now mingled with grief, it grows perhaps the greater.—J. R. R. Tolkien, *The Fellowship of the Ring*

Acting in love

This Sunday we remember how Jesus entered his Passion. Knowing the pain to come, he persisted. According to John's gospel, he did so out of love.

Today's text urges: "let all that you do be done in love." At the close of the letter, Paul builds upon his earlier praise of love (1 Corinthians 13), fully aware that some at Corinth were not acting in love. Paul rounds out the letter by recapping this call to action: let *all* your activity be in love.

Acting in love is not easy. It involves not simply what I *think* is loving, nor whether I *feel* loving in acting. It means acting with others' best interests at heart. It involves doing what may be selfless, hard, and necessary to aid another.

Acting in love is what Christ has first done for us. The call to love, then, is the same as the call to follow Jesus today.

Prayer

Lord, make us instruments of your peace. Where there is hatred, let us sow love; where there is injury, pardon; where there is discord, union; where there is doubt, faith; where there is despair, hope; where there is darkness, light; where there is sadness, joy. Grant that we may not so much seek to be consoled as to console; to be understood as to understand; to be loved as to love. For it is in giving that we receive; it is in pardoning that we are pardoned; and it is in dying that we are born to eternal life. Amen. (Prayer attributed to Francis of Assisi, *ELW*, p. 87)

March 25

1 Corinthians 10:16–17

The cup of blessing that we bless, is it not a sharing in the blood of Christ? The bread that we break, is it not a sharing in the body of Christ? Because there is one bread, we who are many are one body, for we all partake of the one bread.

To ponder

Whether we like it or not, . . . from the time we become a Christian, we are at the same time a member of the Christian church—even if we do not permit our name to be placed on a church roll, even if we refuse to identify ourselves with a particular congregation and share responsibilities with them, even if we absent ourselves from the worship of a congregation. Our membership in the church is a corollary of our faith in Christ.

We can no more be a Christian and have nothing to do with the church than we can be a person and not be in a family.—Eugene H. Peterson, *A Long Obedience in the Same Direction*

Part of a redeemed community

In today's text, Paul's word for "sharing" (*koinōnia*) is a strong word. It means community, communion, fellowship, participation, or a holding in common. It is seen, for one example, in the holding of all things in common practiced by early church communities in Acts.

In Western societies, we often view the Lord's supper individualistically. We prepare ourselves, but as individuals. Paul's focus was more communal. For him, those who come to the Lord's table become full partners in a redeemed community. They join others in connection to Christ. They become not individual Jesus-lovers, but one body in Christ.

You are not alone. In Christ, you are part of something bigger, greater, richer, and more expansive than may ever be realized this side of eternity.

Prayer

Just as this broken bread was scattered upon the mountains and then was gathered together and became one, so may your church be gathered together from the ends of the earth into your kingdom; for yours is the glory and the power through Jesus Christ forever. (Didache 9.4)

March 26

1 Corinthians 10:31–33

Whether you eat or drink, or whatever you do, do everything for the glory of God. Give no offense to Jews or to Greeks or to the church of God, just as I try to please everyone in everything I do, not seeking my own advantage, but that of many, so that they may be saved.

To ponder

A Christian is lord of all, completely free of everything. A Christian is a servant, completely attentive to the needs of all.
—Martin Luther, "The Freedom of a Christian"

Lives of worship

In today's text Paul concludes three chapters of discussing a pressing ethical issue. He summarizes: "do everything for the glory of God," and strive to give no offense to others' faith.

Paul's response suggests there are ethically indifferent matters, as well as non-negotiables. Amid this, Christians are called not to ethical living per se, but to lives of worship—doing "everything for the glory of God." That is, ethics matter because they reflect a response of worship. Related, we are called to "give no offense," which here is not simply refraining from hurting someone's feelings. It means primarily not harming or hindering another's faith. In sum, Paul encourages honoring both God and neighbor, grounded in a freedom that is geared toward worship and service.

Life is messy. So is the world in which we live. Most issues we consider are not clear-cut. In such a world, Paul's word is helpful: do everything for the glory of God, and strive not to give offense to the faith and well-being of others. However general, this reminds us of the overall point: At the end of the day, let your life be one of worship—and your ethics serve your neighbor. That will be enough.

Prayer

Direct us, O God, in all we do so that by the grace of our Lord Jesus Christ, we may be guided and empowered by your Holy Spirit to live lives that worship God with our whole heart and honor our neighbors as ourselves. Amen.

March 27

1 Corinthians 11:18, 20–21, 33

When you come together as a church, I hear that there are divisions among you; . . . When you come together, it is not really to eat the Lord's supper. For when the time comes to eat, each of you goes ahead with your own supper, and one goes hungry and another becomes drunk. . . .

So then, my brothers and sisters, when you come together to eat, wait for one another.

To ponder

For Christians, to share in the Eucharist, the Holy Communion, means to live as people who know that they are always *guests*—that they have been welcomed and that they are wanted.—Rowan Williams, *Being Christian*

Being a guest

Throughout our married life, my wife and I have lived at a distance from family. So, at holidays and other times, we visit them. Although they have visited us, we are most often visitors. We know what it's like to be guests.

Guests don't set the schedule or the guest list. They don't pick the menu or nitpick the selections. They share spaces with others. They adapt to new rhythms. They receive graciously. Although sometimes challenging, being a guest is a life-giving break from the mundane routines we control.

We church people can learn to be better guests. We tend to control things. We tend to nitpick what is given, criticize others in our spaces, and refuse to change. In doing so, we ensure that new guests stay away.

This was a problem at Corinth. Although many issues are present, Paul highlights the reluctance of some "haves" to honor the "have-nots" in the community as true equals. A more contextual translation for "wait for" is "welcome one another genuinely" (v. 33). At Corinth, some had simply forgotten that at Christ's table we are all guests.

Are you a good guest in Christ's house? It involves not just dropping by. He invites you to sit awhile, receive, give up control, join new people, and be changed.

Prayer

Lord Jesus Christ, help us to receive your gifts with gladness. Amen.

March 28 / Maundy Thursday

1 Corinthians 11:23–25

I received from the Lord what I also handed on to you, that the Lord Jesus on the night when he was betrayed took a loaf of bread, and when he had given thanks, he broke it and said, "This is my body that is for you. Do this in remembrance of me." In the same way he took the cup also, after supper, saying, "This cup is the new covenant in my blood. Do this, as often as you drink it, in remembrance of me."

To ponder

And then we gathered around that table . . . and then something outrageous and terrifying happened. Jesus happened to me. I still can't explain my first communion. It made no sense. I was in tears and physically unbalanced: I felt as if I had just stepped off a curb or been knocked over, painlessly, from behind. . . . [It] utterly short-circuited my ability to do anything but cry.—Sara Miles, *Take This Bread*

Jesus invites you

From the very start, church communities have practiced eating together.

Today's text is from our oldest account of the Lord's supper. Just beforehand, Paul's description implies it was not only a ritual act, but a substantive meal (*deipnon*, "supper," verse 20). Early Christians did this not just because shared meals were widely practiced in antiquity. They did it because Jesus told them to.

We often forget the simple truth: just before his Passion, Jesus ate with friends. At his darkest hour, he gathered with others. It says something profound about not only the meal's sacredness, but how highly Jesus values his followers—including us. In his worst of times, Jesus would recline next to you for dinner.

This Maundy Thursday, Jesus invites you to join him at the table. He invites not just you, but others as well. Whether or not you fully understand it, Jesus invites you to eat and drink. Here Christ is given for you.

Prayer

O Christ our Savior, we receive your gifts, acknowledge your love, and trust your mercy. Amen.

March 29 / Good Friday

1 Corinthians 11:26

For as often as you eat this bread and drink the cup, you proclaim the Lord's death until he comes.

To ponder

One has to have a powerful religious imagination to see redemption in the cross, to discover life in death and hope in tragedy. What kind of salvation is that? No human language can fully describe what salvation through the cross means. Salvation through the cross is a mystery and can only be apprehended through faith, repentance, and humility.
—James H. Cone, *The Cross and the Lynching Tree*

The cross is at the heart of our faith

Good Friday is not for the faint of heart.

The day centers on the cross of Christ. It focuses on his death. It highlights a cruel act of capital punishment upon an innocent man who loved unconditionally.

But in the cross, we see who God really is. That's why Paul draws attention to it in 1 Corinthians 11:26, connecting it to the Lord's supper: the bread and cup *proclaim Jesus' death*. The community at Corinth had forgotten this. We tend to forget this as well: at the core of our faith is the cross. Our dearest acts of worship reiterate this fact. At the cross, God is made visible, Jesus saves, and the Holy Spirit creates faith.

Early on as a university professor, Martin Luther had an awakening experience studying Psalm 22. Identifying its words with Christ's from the cross, Luther was struck by how our Savior willingly experienced this deep desperation and alienation from God. In his suffering Christ identified fully with our experience. At the cross the Almighty became the All-merciful. Here the Judge became the Judged. Here the God of justice became the All-loving. In Christ, the One who knew no sin became sin so that we may be saved.

Prayer

O God, in Christ you willingly took on our worst so that we might have and know your best. By the Spirit's power, we embrace and receive all you have done for us in the cross. Amen.

March 30 /
Resurrection of Our Lord

1 Corinthians 15:54–57

"Death has been swallowed up in victory."
"Where, O death, is your victory?
Where, O death, is your sting?"
The sting of death is sin, and the power of sin is the law. But thanks be to God, who gives us the victory through our Lord Jesus Christ.

To ponder

Never let anything so fill you with sorrow as to make you forget the joy of Christ risen.—Mother Teresa, *No Greater Love*

God's way is resurrection

Where I live, winter is cold. Most trees, bushes, and plants drop all greenery and flowers, leaving barrenness. In the dead of winter, it is remarkably hard to imagine these things "living" again.

But spring eventually comes, and life blooms again. Creation itself attests to how God's way is one of resurrection life.

In today's reading, Paul uses language from Isaiah 25:8 and Hosea 13:14 to convey God's victory over death. In doing so, Paul shows the timelessness of the human longing to see an end to death's cruelty and finality.

This is the good news of Easter Sunday: death is conquered. The grave is emptied. Jesus Christ is risen. All our deaths now are temporary pauses.

Much about the resurrection remains a mystery. One thing is not: God has given victory over death to us through Jesus Christ. And so, in response to the message Christ is risen, we rightly respond: "Christ is risen indeed. Alleluia!"

Prayer

"Christ the Lord is ris'n today!"
All on earth with angels say;
raise your joys and triumphs high;
sing, O heav'ns; and earth, reply.
(ELW 373)

Notes

February 14: Dion DiMucci, in "Dion Is Still a New York Guy at Heart," *AP News*, July 26, 2016, https://apnews.com/article/entertainment-music-new-york-paul-simon-dion-dimucci-052d666fc 434490ca748057c51222d95. Imposition of ashes: *ELW*, p. 254. **February 15:** Marta Mrotek, *Miracle in Progress* (Scotts Valley, CA: CreateSpace, 2014). **February 16:** Audre Lorde, *Sister Outsider* (New York: Penguin, 2020). **February 17:** St. Francis de Sales, "Treatise on the Love of God," *Catholic Treasury*, www.catholictreasury.info/books/on_love_of_God/lg191.php. **February 18:** Albert Einstein, *Einstein on Cosmic Religion and Other Opinions and Aphorisms* (New York: Dover 2009), 53. **February 19:** James Cone, "An African-American Perspective on the Cross and Suffering," in Jacob Tesfai, ed., *The Scandal of a Crucified World* (New York: Orbis, 1994), 58. **February 20:** Elizabeth Johnson, *She Who Is* (New York: Crossroad, 1993), 163. **February 21:** Mitri Raheb, *Faith in the Face of Empire* (Maryknoll, NY: Orbis, 2014), 127. **February 22:** Octavia Butler, *Parable of the Talents* (New York: Seven Stories, 1998), 41. **February 23:** Emmy Kegler, *One Coin Found* (Minneapolis: Fortress, 2019), 176. **February 24:** Deesha Philyaw, *The Secret Lives of Church Ladies* (Morgantown, WV: West Virginia University, 2020), 10. **February 25:** Gregory Boyle, *Tattoos on the Heart* (New York: Free, 2011), 39. **February 26:** Gordon D. Kaufman, *In Face of Mystery* (Cambridge, MA: Harvard University, 1993), 51. **February 27:** Martin Luther, "The Blessed Sacrament of the Holy and True Body of Christ, and the Brotherhoods," in *The Annotated Luther*, vol. 1 (Minneapolis: Fortress, 2015). **February 28:** Hector Xtravaganza, as recollected by Jose Disla Xtravaganza, in "A Glittering Goodbye to Hector Xtravaganza," *The New York Times*, March 11, 2019. **February 29:** Carl Sandburg, *Remembrance Rock* (New York: Harcourt, Brace & Company, 1948), 7. **March 1:** Steve Jobs, commencement address, Stanford University, June 12, 2005. **March 2:** Marriage, *ELW*, 288. **March 3:** Assata Shakur, "To My People," letter from prison, July 4, 1973. **March 4:** Ethel Waters and Charles Samuels, *His Eye Is on the Sparrow* (New York: Doubleday, 1951). **March 5:** Text: © 2017 Paul D. Weber, b. 1949, admin. Augsburg Fortress; ACS 1048, st. 3. **March 6:** Text: Cathy Skogen-Soldner, b. 1956; © 1999 Augsburg Fortress; ELW 453, st. 4. **March 7:** Text: Anne Krentz Organ, b. 1960, © 2020 Augsburg Fortress; "This Is Christ's Body," ACS 967. **March 8:** Text: John Fawcett, 1740–1817, alt., "Blest Be the Tie That Binds," ELW 656, st. 3. **March 9:** Frederick Buechner, *Wishful Thinking* (London: Collins, 1973), 122. **March 10:** Meister Eckhart, trans. Maurice O'C Walshe, *The Complete Mystical Works of Meister Eckhart* (New York: Herder & Herder, 2010), 62. **March 11:** Martin Luther King Jr., *Strength to Love* (Philadelphia: Fortress, 1981), 53. **March 12:** William Shakespeare, *The Complete Works of William Shakespeare* (New York: Avenil, 1975), 1210. March 13: Sarah S. Scherschligt, *God Holds You* (Self-published, 2022), 16. **March 14:** Meta Herrick Carlson, *Ordinary Blessings for Parents* (Minneapolis: Broadleaf, 2022), 119. **March 15:** Cole Arthur Riley, *This Here Flesh* (Hodder & Stoughton, 2022), 57. **March 16:** Rachel Held Evans, *Searching for Sunday* (Nashville: Thomas Nelson, 2015), 208–9. **March 17:** N. K. Jemisin, *The City We Became* (London: Orbit, 2020), 233. **March 18:** Arianne Braithwaite Lehn, *Ash and Starlight* (Des Peres, MO: Chalice, 2019), 118. **March 19:** Kayla Craig, *To Light Their Way* (Carol Stream, IL: Tyndale Momentum, 2021), 28. **March 20:** Silvia Moreno-Garcia, *The Daughter of Doctor Moreau* (New York: Del Rey, 2022), 302. **March 21:** Robin Wall Kimmerer, *Braiding Sweetgrass* (Minneapolis: Milkweed, 2013), 104. **March 22:** Howard Thurman, *Meditations of the Heart* (Boston: Beacon, 2022), 77–78. **March 23:** Sara Miles, *Take This Bread* (New York: Ballantine, 2008), xvi. Prayer from *ELW*, 284. **March 24:** J. R. R. Tolkien, *The Lord of the Rings, Part One: The Fellowship of the Ring* (New York: Ballantine, 1965), 452. Prayer from *ELW*, 85. **March 25:** Eugene H. Peterson, *A Long Obedience in the Same Direction*, 2nd ed. (Downers Grove, IL: InterVarsity, 2000), 175. "Didache" prayer from *The Apostolic Fathers*, 3rd ed., ed. and trans. Michael W. Holmes (Grand Rapids: Baker, 2007). **March 26:** Martin Luther, "The Freedom of a Christian," trans. Mark Tranvik, in *Martin Luther's Basic Theological Writings*, 3rd ed., eds. Timothy F. Lull and William R. Russell (Minneapolis: Fortress, 2012), 404. **March 27:** Rowan Williams, *Being Christian* (Grand Rapids: Eerdmans, 2014), 41. Emphasis original. **March 28:** Sara Miles, *Take This Bread: A Radical Conversion* (New York: Ballantine, 2008), 58–59. **March 29:** James H. Cone, *The Cross and the Lynching Tree* (Maryknoll, MD: Orbis, 2013), 157–8. **March 30:** Mother Teresa, *No Greater Love* (Novato, CA: New World Library, 1997), 137. Text: Charles Wesley, 1707–1788, alt.; ELW 373, "Christ the Lord Is Risen Today!," sts. 1, 4, and 6.